BAD TIMING

CROSSWORDS WERE NEVER RUMPELSTILTSKIN'S THING

PAPARAZZI CATCH CINDERELLA SHOPPING AT PAYLESS SHOES

THE EMPEROR DROPS OFF HIS OLD CLOTHES AT GOODWILL

A TOUGH CHOICE FOR TED

THINGS GOT A LITTLE CONFUSING WITH THE NEW GUY AT THE MINE

HOW HUMPTY DUMPTY ACTUALLY SURVIVED

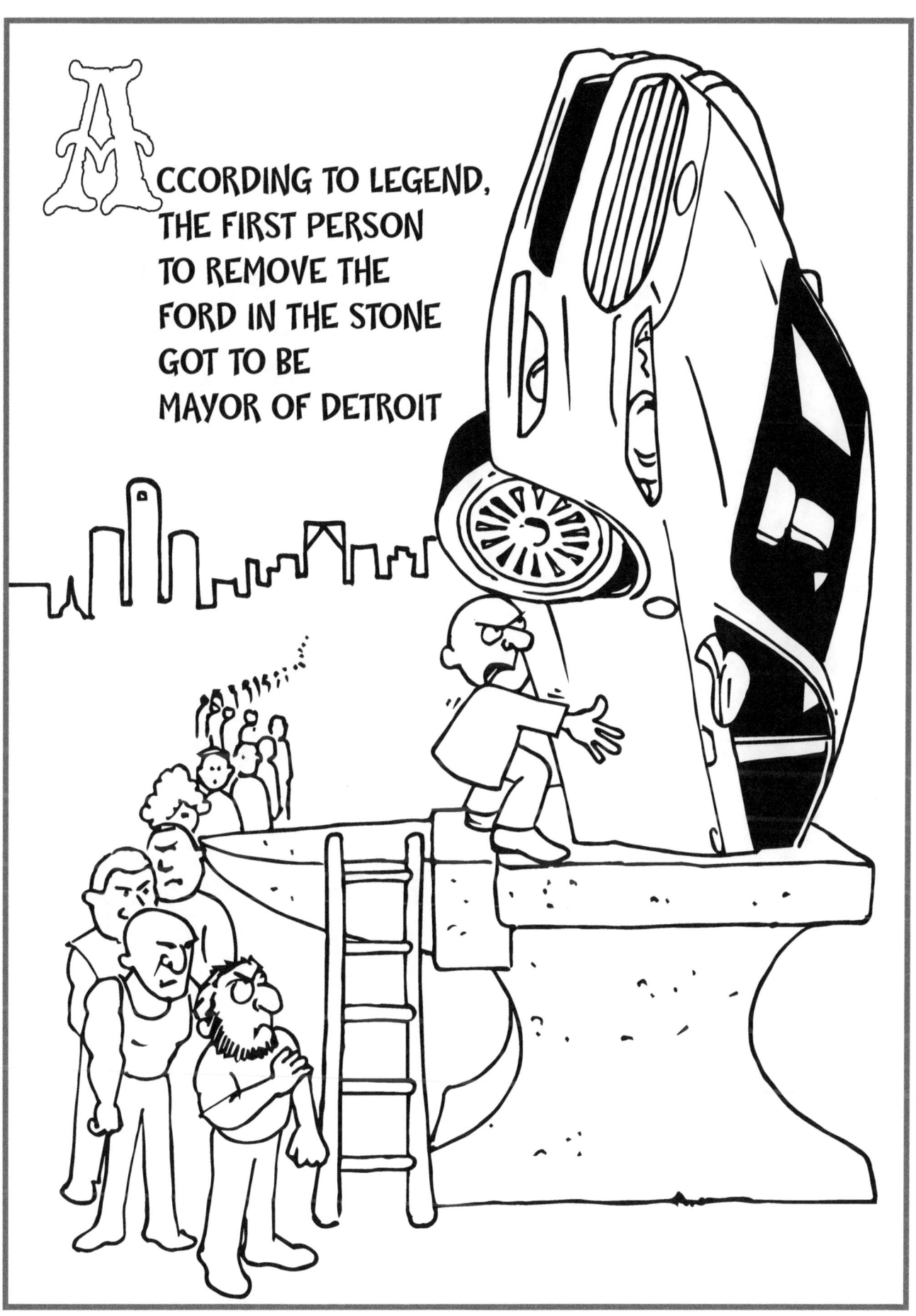

A ROUGH DAY FOR PINOCCHIO IN WOOD SHOP

RUMPELSTILTSKIN CALLS TRIP TO SIX FLAGS "PRETTY BORING"

THE PRINCE HAS AN IDEA

THE EMPEROR'S NEW CAR

SHAZAM! A boisterous and excessively cheery woman appears out of nowhere to shower Cinderella with unexpected gifts. So this was either her Fairy Godmother, or maybe Oprah. Unclear.

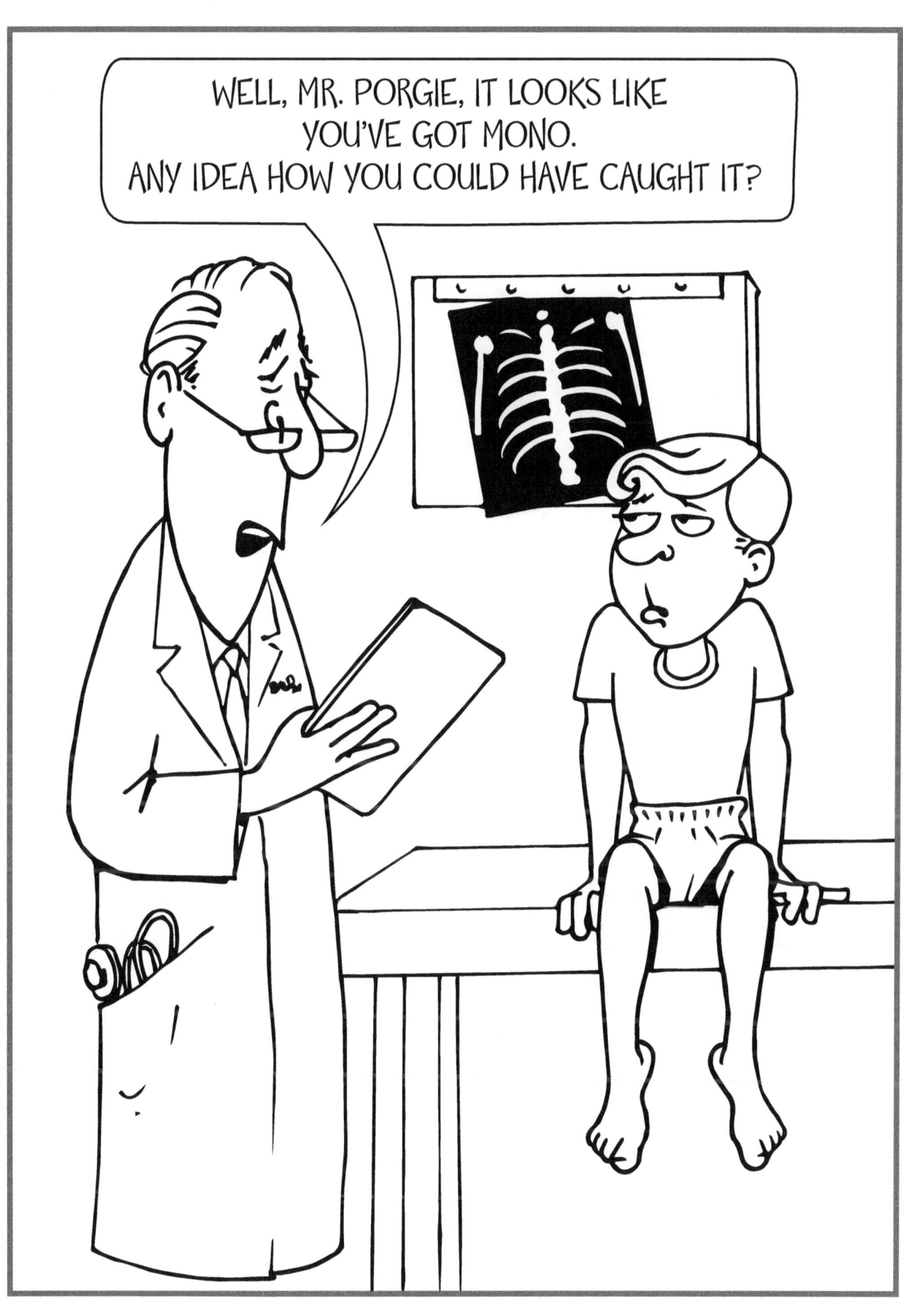

JOHN HENRY LEARNS THERE'S MORE THAN ONE WAY TO MAKE A TUNNEL

MARY OBTAINS RESTRAINING ORDER AGAINST STALKER LAMB

**THIS DAY IN HISTORY:
AFTER HOLDING IT FOR TWENTY YEARS, LESSER-KNOWN
RIP VAN TINKLE FINALLY USES THE RESTROOM.**

NEVER AGAIN WOULD A JUNGLE LIGHTNING STORM DENY SHERE KHAN HIS DELICIOUS MOWGLI DINNER

RUDOLPH'S NOSE NO LONGER RED:
CREDITS SWITCH TO TWO-PLY TISSUE